Pub 7.68

Distributed in the USA by Harper & Row
and in Canada by Book Center, Montreal

© 1980 by Fulvio Testa. First American edition published in 1983 by Peter Bedrick Books, 239 Central Park West,
New York, N.Y. 10024. Published by agreement with Andersen Press Ltd., London. All rights reserved.
ISBN 0-911745-01-7. Printed in Italy by Grafiche AZ, Verona. LC 83-71163

LEAVES

Fulvio Testa

English text by Naomi Lewis

Peter Bedrick Books
New York

Autumn came.
The leaves turned red and gold and flame.

One leaf dropped,
as many leaves had done before.
Soon there would be more.

See it float through the air,
swing lightly, hover...
No hurry! Take your time!
Your dance will soon be over
Soundless as feather
leaf meets the ground.
But what has he found?

'Why, there is my friend!
And another! Another!
My sister! My brother!'
All the leaves greet him,
rustling together,
joyful to meet him.

'We wondered about you,
were quite sad without you.
But tell us the news!'
So they spoke of past days,
told their memories, their views.

'I miss the friendly ants,'
murmured a voice.
'How often they would meet,
bring gossip, scramble about
on busy tickling feet
that made no noise.
In my mind I see them well.'

How many are there? Can you tell?

'I like to think of how
we fed the caterpillar,
hid the chrysalis,
welcomed the butterfly –
Who could forget that day!
Every leaf watched
as the blue one hatched,
spread its bright wings,
flew away.'

'There was a bird – remember?
A lark? A nightingale?
Touching down on a bough
it sang to us, time without number.
Where does it shelter now?'

'Yes, and where
are those summer wanderers,
creatures of the air,
the little moths and flies,
our daily visitors?'

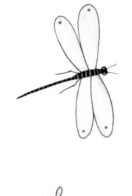

'But autumn came.'
'Too soon,' a sad leaf said.
'We turned from green to flame,
to brown and gold.
The wind blew cold.
We fell. Our tale was told,
and that's our fate.'

'But wait –
not all leaves fall,' said a newcomer.
'Yonder, a tree shines green
as if in summer.
Now that seems curious.'

'Ah yes,' a leaf replied,
'the evergreen, a tree mysterious,
they say, a wise one too.
It lives through every season.
Perhaps there is a reason.
I wish we knew.'

The sad leaf said, 'Yet see
the empty branches of our tree,
how bleak and bare.
If only we were there.'

'Wait,' said the evergreen.
'Though you lie here in the ground,
your adventures are not over.
In time, in time,
in tree and flower you will be found
as you will discover.'

Spring came,
brought the warm sun
and the light hours,
and all the tree's branches showed
new buds and flowers.
How bright,
how magical a sight.

The evergreen too
often paused to admire.
(Who looked at him now
in the flowering season?)
Thick-leaved, like a forest,
growing deeper and higher,
not winner, not loser,
he kept hid within him
till his own time was due –
(best seen in bad weather,
the stormy, the frozen) –
his own dark green fire.